Leadership
A collection of essays

Followership:
The Manual

You are
here

by J. Michael Dumoulin

*To Tom, Rob, John, Dom, and
all of the bosses I've ever had who themselves had
difficult bosses. Thanks for the privilege of
learning from you.*

Fourth edition

ISBN 979-8-8693-6397-8

Design by Garnett
Distributed by Labrynth

Table of contents

*For more information about the author;
to comment about the book; or submit personal
examples and stories or new
tenets about Followership for future
updates and revisions, visit:*

jmichaeldumoulin.com

Chapter 1
Introduction

You've never heard of me; there's no reason that you should have but I enable my boss and make her successful. Your boss doesn't know me—he's never heard of me either—and chances are he'll never figure out that his program won't or can't work without me. Not me personally, of course, but the figurative, collective me. I'm the one person who always seems to be on the team who makes things happen. I watch and anticipate. I plug in, inflate or grease things when it's necessary. Not because I'm told to, but because I care and it's the right thing to do.

I'm a follower, but not just any subordinate. I'm THE follower. If noticed, I might be described as that really, really good deputy, "his right arm man" or "best girl Friday ever." Maybe I'm referred to as "the #1 #2." More than likely, though, I'm invisible and things just seem to succeed around me. What doesn't have a label doesn't exist, so I stay invisible and that's okay with me. Scientists will tell you that the very act of illuminating or measuring something as small and insignificant as an atom will change it. I'm like that: strong and binding, in fact elemental to an organization, but living unseen in the nano-weeds. Too much attention or recognition, though, introduces variables I can't manage, perhaps resistance or resentment from other nanos around me. Distractions like that weaken my influence.

The military academies have an axiom: "To be a good leader, you must first learn to be a good follower." The sentiment is prevalent in such institutions that break down leaders to build back followers so they can become leaders.

But it's also said (even in the military academies) that everyone has a boss. So, if everyone has a boss, then to some degree everyone is a follower. Most people we think of as leaders are just high-powered followers, intent on providing THEIR boss — whomever it might be — optimal results from the resources and people in their portfolio. Sometimes the effort comes at a tremendous cost to the pool of resources and people they've been given. The truly effective follower husbands, grows, and sharpens the amount and quality of those resources, their abilities to influence, and the people they must rely on so that they can provide the boss — again, whomever it might be — with the maximum value when and where that boss needs it. The truly effective follower must strategically and tactically anticipate, motivate, plan, and manage. All of these things are leadership traits.

That's why to be a good follower you have to already possess good leadership traits. The only real difference between good subordinates and good leaders is the scope of resources and people they've been assigned. Or in other words, the amount of trouble they can get into in a given period of time.

Chapter 2
A broader definition

Followership isn't a concept that necessarily only applies to a direct succession or an obvious chain of command. You could argue that if a follower has a choice—and I believe that's exactly the point of this book—then she gets to decide who or what to follow. Forget Charles Manson: what if what she's chosen to follow isn't a person? What if it's the Constitution of the United States, or the Ten Commandments? Imagine the jumping of protocol or the apparent chaos this causes in the minds and plans of appointed or rising leaders!

Following a non-person isn't a bad thing. When a six-up or six-in-hand team of horses or oxen pulls a cart, the hames, trace, and shaft connect the beasts' pulling force to the machine, not the driver. When a team of horses is lined up, every set of horses out in front of the first one contributes its energy back to the wagon, tied together through a series of harnesses and crossbars. The reigns may run up to the front two but the strongest pair of animals is always on the tongue closest to the wagon to physically steer and brake it. Imagine what a mess it would be if every animal pulled and stopped the wagon only with ropes and the wagon master held a set for each beast. The driver on the cart would spend all of his time untangling rope. It's a good analogy in the sense that a follower's allegiance to broader concepts transfers order, predictability, and motivation back to the leader without the mess of that leader having to create and manage it separately for every follower.

"Followers" and "following" are as different from "followership" as simply being at the front of the line is different from motivating others in the line to step forward or deliberately affecting the direction of the march. Barbara Kellerman noted in a December 2007 Harvard Business Review article "What Every Leader Needs to Know about Followers" that scholars on followership (and yes, there actually have been a few) classify subordinates into four or five types depending on such things as how motivated they are to make change, how much they care about the welfare of others, and their level of independence. She noted that executive business coach Ira Chaleff even classifies followers by how willing they are to tell the boss off, although she more delicately describes it as "the degree to which the follower challenges the leader." In general, though, it seems the experts peg followers on a sliding scale from "zombie" to someplace just below "leader." Great followership is on the extreme edge of the caring and engagement end of that spectrum, and like leadership, has developed some rules based on what seems to work.

The degree of followership abilities, like loyalties, is usually obvious in individuals if you know to look for it. But like loyalties, sometimes it can jump levels, fade to invisibility, or be tied to the wagon of conventions or ideals that a leader sits on, not to the leader himself. Sorting out a reliable network of followers can be a messy task for a leader who is trying to calculate the strengths of his team. A follower can make it easier on a leader—a sub-point to this book—through consistent, reliable, forward-moving actions (referred to in Chapter 4 simply as "integrity").

Chapter Three
Great followers

Some of the strongest or most memorable lessons about followership can be found in popular literature. You don't have to cast far to find great fictional seconds. C. S. Forester, for example, invented Captain Horatio Hornblower's Lieutenant Bush. Herman Melville brought us Starbuck, the faithful, stalwart, levelheaded first mate on the whaling ship Pequod captained by the mad Captain Ahab. These authors and scores more didn't find their examples reading leadership books. The kernels of their characters came from real life, probably from direct observation.

So, if they could see great followership traits and write about them in made-up people, why don't the rest of us notice or talk more about followership? Why isn't "followership" as salient as "leadership?"

Take this test for yourself. Conduct a simple online search for "quotes about leadership." My search found 77,400,000 results. Then, search on "quotes about followership." My query brought up 212,000, or just less than three-tenths of one percent, or one followership cite for every 365 citations about leaders.

History books, magazine articles, and news broadcasts are filled with stories about great, interesting, and not-so-great leaders. Some are fiction and some are true, but most are incomplete in the sense that through necessary brevity, the lessons taught us and the accomplishments we remember of these leaders usually leave out the follower's role. We take for granted that a great leader did something great because people followed him, of course, but we usually forget that at the start, and during critical points in the revolution orchestrated by that leader, some lieutenant facilitated, implemented, cajoled, sacrificed, or otherwise convinced others that standing with the leader was a good thing.

We read about the exploits of Alexander the Great, but few have studied General Parmenion who had first served Alex's father, Phillip, and stayed on to quietly offer the boy king conventional strategies that gave balance and wisdom to the conqueror's brash but innovative and brilliant leadership. And what about the poor Greek scribes and horse-holders left behind to rule Alexander's growing string of new capitols and governments? What were those bureaucrats' names? Exactly: I rest my case.

In science and American industry, no one disputes the sheer genius of Thomas Edison, not only because of his inventiveness, but because he was able to mass-deliver practical benefits from his inventions. Few people, however, will ever read about William H. Austin, superintendent of installation at Edison's Brockton electric light operation, or about Francis Upton and Charles Batchelor from Edison's Menlo Park experiments in 1878 and 1879. You'd be hard pressed to argue that Edison's place in history would be as high or revered without such men.

Eberhard Rees, when asked about his long-standing relationship with Werner von Braun said simply, with some humor, "I have to do the dirty work." Rees was von Braun's trusted second for practically all things related to rocket engineering, and Dr. Ernst Stulinger had that role for all things scientific. While von Braun was unquestionably a persuasive leader, it was these two followers and others like them who interpreted, anticipated, and turned von Braun's leadership into the actionable tasks that took the first three men to the moon.

In the early 1900s, Clara Barton convinced two presidents of the United States to establish the American Red Cross, but while she was lobbying for their support in Washington, it was her assistant and trusted advisor Dr. Julian Hubbell, one of the American Red Cross's first disaster relief field agents, who actually managed the new organization's first few challenges. Decades before that, Florence Nightingale's thirty-four nurses followed her into the terrible hospital conditions of the Crimean War to become the "Angels of the Crimea."

Followership has been around, in both good and evil forms, since Eve first said to Adam, "Trust me; it'll be alright just this once." All along the way, the role of the follower has been overshadowed by the charisma of the leader. We need great leaders, so that's okay. Just know, though, that during all that time, great followers have observed, noted, tested, and refined some unspoken lessons—almost doctrine—about the leaders they chose to follow.

Chapter Four
Thirty-six tenets

While doctrine is a bit strong when applied to followership, it's a close description. Doctrine implies an organized group is holding an organized set of intractable beliefs. A more accurate word might be "tenets," which refers to the core principles behind the doctrine. Without the benefits of a lodge and secret handshakes to bind them and coded scrolls of rules to pass down, followers have had to self-reliantly uncover and collect the pages of their tenets as they went along. Here are a few.

Tenet 1
Leaders are called; followers are drafted

If effective followers have all the same skills as effective leaders—just in smaller doses—then followers already posses the dormant seeds of leadership. People grant leadership and can take it away if the leader proves inept. Yes, even in a corporate setting. Leaders "own" the rarified air, but great followers own the dirt. I don't just mean that they know where the bosses asked them to bury the bodies. Followers' hands are calloused from digging all day long. They already know the hired help and understand the weather. What better person is there to lead? A great follower shouldn't be afraid to step up and act when asked.

Tenet 2
Don't do as you're told

A leader's deepest fear, besides no one listening, is that their followers will do exactly what the leader tells them to do. To paraphrase General George Patton, if everyone is thinking the same thing, 'then someone ain't thinkin.' Use your ears and your brains to understand what the boss really wants to accomplish. Then do what's right for your organization. Generations of people depend on you. That's right, generations. It's not just about your fellow followers, managers, and leaders. It's about their families, and children to come. If your organization is going to truly make a difference, it will have an impact felt for generations.

Tenet 3
Integrity

Integrity isn't a concept. It's as real as the forces on the struts and stays of a geodesic dome. Just as a full can of soda is stronger than an empty one and

the kinetic energy latent in the Hoover Dam pushes back against Lake Mead's water pressure to a state of balance, the physical definition behind the ethical and moral attribute is about soundness. In mechanical terms, integrity is a management of forces. In engineering design, it's a balance of reliability and maintainability. In systems terms, it's the ability of materials, equipment and structures to withstand loads against defects and damage. Whether large or minute, continual force and vigilance establishes and maintains Integrity. Yes, now I'm talking about the ethical attribute, not the physical one.

As you manage every application of good followership against the loads and defects of chaos and change, do the right thing. Integrity—holding to your values—above all else makes a Great Follower. Never, ever sacrifice your integrity. As a follower vulnerable to the whims of the leader, sometimes it's all you have to cash in on at the end of the day.

Tenet 4
Do the right thing...quietly

When a captain disregards his ship builders' advice, wise boatwrights will freely help other captains and crews to build seaworthy ships so that someone, anyone, will be out there in the deep ocean for the rescue when the seams of the foolish captain's boat start to leak.

When the rescuers come to save the foolish captain, a wise follower shouldn't expect a thank you, either from the captain or the crew. While august universities give out scholarships based on demonstrated leadership skills, not one would consider followership noteworthy. Town squares are filled with equine statues of great leaders, but nothing is said of the enabling great follower who helped that leader onto his horse.

Leaders can suffer from the "You work for me; I own you" plantation mentality. Experienced followers look past that and understand the attitude for what it is: an insecure posture of power. Not that you should point that out, of course, but being underappreciated can be liberating. Not liberating in the sense that it feels good but literally: without all the attention, a good follower has more freedom to move around.

Quiet humbleness, the subservient attitude, the standing in the shadows while the leader takes the bows, perhaps it's those traits that differentiate leaders and good followers. A leader has to be seen but a follower has to be silent and already in place to grab a loose rein or nail down a loose board before such things become trouble. A proselytizing follower, or one seen by everyone to be in the right place all the time—well, they call that person a leader. Petty jealousies from captains or crews or the belief that the leader knows how to build a better boat simply because the leader is the leader can prevent followers from getting where they know they need to be when they need to be there. So, quiet and invisible: these are the secret traits of great followers.

Tenet 5
Mega plans are evil

Sometimes the most celebrated and praised leaders have the biggest plans. Even if the boss has presented a complicated plan, however, a smart follower keeps the implementation simple.

From a leader's perspective, there is nothing wrong with a giant, complicated plan. It's what they pay leaders for. From a follower's point of view, however, a complicated plan is a minefield in a maze. Worse than that, a follower's convoluted tactics to implement a leader's mega-plan is like crossing that same minefield in the dark.

If they wait for a leader to find consensus on a mega-plan, a follower asked to implement that plan will 1) never have all the details to ensure its success and 2) always be behind and unresponsive to timely opportunities.

General George Marshall once said of his soldiers, "Army officers are intelligent. Give them the bare tree, let them supply the leaves." A good leader should trust frontline followers to build short-term functional plans and give them time to execute them. But good followers don't always work for good leaders.

A good follower who has been asked to accomplish a goal immediately devises a plan. Usually that plan will need people, money and tools. Think of a mega-plan as a giant meal that must be prepared and then eaten. Effective followers study the menu AND the cook. When "Chef" is making resource and timing decisions in the kitchen, the cooks and sous chefs won't have control of a great many variables for long, if ever. If the chef came up through the ranks to become "Chef," presumably this kitchen leader remembers all of the processes, resources and time "Staff" needs to accomplish a masterpiece. But sometimes thestaff isn't given the tools they need to help the leader prepare the meal, or the ute nsils guests will need to eat it. When that happens, the wise follower shoots for simple solutions and lots of incremental or small successes. If the leader doesn't keep this in mind, the follower should: the goal isn't the masterpiece meal, it's a satisfied, happy, healthy guest.

Tenet 6
Pay attention to the words

You've heard the phrase "Choose your words wisely?" A leader's task is to prod up an unexplored path -- prod from the front of the line, mind you --an unruly team lined behind him (or her). It takes some convincing of the masses. A leader who is coaxing actions from his followers is selling those actions. A wise follower has to listen to the words carefully. Leaders use words deliberately; good followers should know how to analyze and interpret those words correctly.

Whenever a leader uses words such as "Truth" and "Right," understand that those concepts are subjective. "Fact" should be verified. A wise follower knows that the three words are not synonymous.

Likewise, when evaluating people's positions on the boss's proposal, don't confuse "Faith," "Hope," and "Confidence." Hope is an unsubstantiated expectation of a positive outcome. It's often the strongest card and the last to be played in most people's hand of coping strategies. Faith is the same expectation, but leaned against a set of previously established rules, promises or doctrine. "Leaned" is an appropriate word, since faith can be a strong wall that either supports and shelters us or blocks our view forward. For many people, though—maybe most people—it's Faith's previous experiences, stories, and history that provide comfort and reassurance. "Confidence," on the other hand, is an analysis of facts and previous trends and an expectation that momentum will carry both to a conclusion at some predictable point in the future. Confidence assumes the analysis is objective, the facts complete, the trends dissected correctly, and the timing well understood. That's a lot of variables and calculations to weigh. Sometimes, it's just easier for some people to hope.

Remember, too, to discern if a leader is trying to resolve or fix a problem. "Fixing a problem" and "resolving a problem" are not the same things. The former focuses on the symptoms of the conflict; the latter the cause. If the water in the bucket is too low, I can fix it by adding more water or resolve the problem by plugging the leak.

Tenet 7
Mediocrity breeds mediocrity

If spontaneous generation is a proven myth, so too is the belief that excellence can come from mediocrity. Mediocrity comes from mediocrity. This applies to organizations that give interview and hiring authority to people of average-to-poor technical skills, job knowledge, creativity, motivations, vision, or education.

If the axiom "grow or die" applies, such organizational cultures are destined to slowly atrophy. To compensate for or hide mediocrity, some companies can quickly adjust their work force (i.e., fire less-productive employees to adjust to a more effective competitor) but organizations with policies of longevity or tenure such as schools, governments, and family-run companies are doomed to stagnate if they restrict new ideas, energy, and processes.

Helen Keller wrote, "The world is moved not only by the mighty shoves of heroes, but also by the aggregate of the tiny pushes of each honest worker." Ever wonder how much better things would be if every one of those workers was just a little more skilled, a little more conscientious, a little wiser, or more honest?

Tenet 8
The 80–17–3 meter

In my experience, eighty out of every hundred people you work with come to work wanting to make a difference and are willing to work or sacrifice within reason to make it happen. Another seventeen will do what's required but don't really care about the mission, not because the work is unimportant, but because in their lives something else is more important. They're still motivated, just not at work. And then there's the three percent who will work against work. These three people probably already have found each other and are actively plotting against you and the 80 percent.

The battleground lines are invisible but if you want to get anything accomplished at work, you're fighting a tug-of-war with the 3 percent to win support from the 80 and 17 percent. It's you against three; the odds that you will succeed are poor at best so brace yourself in advance for resistance.

Every situation will have a different "normal." Maybe it's 90-8-2 (clicking on almost all cylinders) or 60-35-5 (near total chaos). The proportions will vary. The key is to find your normal, then with situational awareness figure out how you're doing. Fluctuations in the normal may mean invisible, external forces are at work—morale is high, stress is low, and so on.

Tenet 9
Do "The Dirty"

No, not THAT Dirty. The dirty work. The dirty work your leader doesn't, won't, or can't take the time to do but that is critical to his or her (and your) success. Dirty work like building and maintaining relationships between people both internal and external to the team. And no, not THAT kind of relationship.

All work is done by workers. It's the follower with one foot in his boss's tent and the other around his peers' campfires who understands the work force. Nurture this connection. Most bosses don't have the bandwidth to lead strategically AND interact one-on-one. Every person is a novel worth reading; their story is an adventure and the lessons they've collected over a lifetime are a treasure chest of insight for a good follower.

Just as a bridge's foundation is often invisible in the fog, the strength that turns a decision into real change comes from the unseen gray areas closer to ground level. The human element is an enigma hiding in a sanctuary where most leaders aren't allowed, or are just uninterested in visiting.

While the leader is looking down asking, "Just how much will that pier hold?" the human element holding up the bridge is asking "Is that guy going to jump, or what?"

Think about it: if a leader's responsibility is to figure out where the ship should go and make sure it gets there at any or all costs, you and the rest of the followers can't be sure that the boss won't throw a few crewmen out of the dirigible along the way. Having to look behind all the time to make sure someone's not tossed overboard changes people. It affects commitment, buy-in to the mission at hand, the level of time and enthusiasm they are willing to sign up for, and more.

Team interactions, personal issues, voids in skills or job knowledge, and a million other people-factors positively or negatively impact the quality and timeline of every decision the boss makes every day. While a strategic leader should know that, followers MUST know the workers around them intimately if they are to have reasonable expectations about delivering whatever the boss asks. And, no, not that kind of "intimately," either.

Tenet 10
Leverage your loyalty

The degree of usefulness a follower is to his leader depends, in part, on how influential the leader allows the follower to become. Most leaders don't GIVE away the ability to influence so a great follower needs to home-grow it as they would a Victory Garden with crops like Integrity, Hard Work, Accuracy, and Loyalty. Once acknowledged—or even unacknowledged but seen by other leaders—the ability to be useful has value. So in that sense, like integrity, loyalty is an asset, a commodity.

The more assets a follower has, the more options she has, too: options to help the leader she's chosen or options to choose another leader to help. Options are only assets, however, if the follower is willing or prepared to exercise them.

At least in the U.S., today's workers can "vote with their feet." But slaves can't vote, so an effective follower always has to be prepared to cut the chains and move on. If they can't, they've abdicated their leverage. It might mean putting personal financial matters in order, preparing the family for change, or massaging contacts. Some followers I knew in the military rented and never bought a house for this very reason. They were always ready to move on. A bit extreme, perhaps, but you get the point.

Tenet 11
Passion

Angry young men and women lose years of momentum in their work years looking at how things SHOULD be, not how they ARE. The passion is admirable and for some, "SHOULD be" motivates but for many it just embitters and frustrates. Eventually employers and supervisors remove those workers—especially if they engage with the customer—like a gardener prunes less productive limbs from a fruit tree.

So if you're one of the Angry, what should you do? Obviously, choosing to be happy and settling for what you have is an option but you have to first recognize the anger, then give it up. To many, that smacks of compromise and that just won't do. For the angry young man (or woman), the only solution is to make AND execute a plan to move on. That takes research, contacts, planning... and time. If spouses, family, financial or other commitments are part of the equation, it also takes courage, acceptance of emotional support, and a willingness to recognize the anger for its weaknesses and strengths.

Tenet 12
Neutral buoyancy

Aptitude in any organization rises to a natural level of neutral buoyancy. In other words, an organization has levels of ineptitudes. What clouds the water, of course, is that everyone's aptitude limitations are different so the boundary layers aren't as clear as leaders would like—

otherwise they would know where, and how thick those levels go. With ineptitude comes insecurity, and with insecurity often comes defensiveness.

All that is a long way of getting to the point that when it comes to passion—the good kind, not the kind that embitters—a person's emotional connection to the mission or tasks at hand can get stuck beneath a boundary layer of ineptitude. Passion and enthusiasm have incredible, uplifting power, so the more obvious these are, the more they may be seen as threats and the more passive pushback they seem to get. Maybe even active resistance. A leader looking down from above that layer may not feel it or see it.

A follower is often either below the boundary layer, in it, or hovering just above it and is therefore closer to being able to help a passionate person rise. Why should you care? You should care because every organization needs enthusiastic, committed people willing to push the mission harder, faster and with more quality. And because that passion is often the seed inside a future leader. And because if the enthusiasm doesn't find a state of neutral buoyancy above that layer of static aptitude, it WILL dissipate or move along the layer like an air bubble under the ice, until it finds a path up someplace else. If what you're doing is important, isn't it important to have good, committed people beside you while you're doing it?

Tenet 13
Teamwork is so last century

Bosses and HR departments only looking for employees who will "take one for the team" or "be a team player" or even "work well with others" pass over more than half of the U.S. population: those who don't thrive on teams, or those who are too individualistic or too focused to compromise.

Yes, I'm talking about the introvert who finds interacting with a team exhausting, exasperating, loud and chaotic. Being part of a team is a little about communications and a lot about compromise, both personal and organizational. While compromise widens application, it's a killer when applied to new creative thought. Revolutionary ideas are more likely to come from that quiet person in the back who was looking out the window, or facing the corner, or looking at the cockroach scurrying along the baseboard--not from safe, sanitized, civilized discussions cooked up around a meeting table. While team harmony is a leader's charge, a great follower's job is to nurture the loner, the misfit, the shy and intimidated. A leader can't afford to spend time on these individuals but an organization can't afford to ignore them.

Tenet 14
Being wrong

Every good follower dreads the day the boss is convinced he's right when the follower knows he's wrong or worse, when the follower knows from experience that there's a better way but the boss just won't listen. The boss may be wrong, but she's still the boss. With the willingness and courage to lead out front comes the privilege of getting it wrong, and if she's fortunate enough, the courtesy of surviving to get it right the next time.

It's tempting sometimes for a follower to just throw up her hands and say, "Fine, you want to do it that way? Well, then, let the consequences be on your head." That's an attitude often rooted in frustration and fatigue. If the boss is going to be wrong—and especially if you know it—that's when he's going to need you most. A plan to minimize the damage may be in both of your best interests.

Hopefully, it's not a plan the follower ever has to execute. Whether you call it a branch plan, or a sequel, or "follow-on actions," pulling together all the parts of that Plan B in tangent to the leader's decision can become a delicate dance. Remember Tenet 4 and do the right thing quietly lest you lose your leader's trust.

For a great follower, not having a Plan B is itself a plan. Barbara Kellerman in her Harvard Business Review article wrote that the hallmark of a good follower is their willingness to act and it's true that usually Tenet One—not being afraid to act—trumps the "deer in the headlights" approach. However, inaction or the withholding of action can be a powerful tool on the belt if used sparingly.

One benefit of following is that an out-front leader will always be first in the line of fire, proportionally leaving more followers around at the end of the day than good leaders. The downsides to a follower for being wrong are, frankly, whatever consequences come with being on the losing side of any argument. Like starting even the most justified mutiny, if you intend to disobey leadership, make sure the issue 1) is worth the potential cost and 2) is one you can win.

Tenet 15
Great followers don't lead: they shepherd

Cowboys and shepherds don't own their herds; they're just personally responsible for everything about them. It takes a lot of talent (and energy) for a great follower to steer his charges from the rear with dogs or a big stick.

It's better (and less exhausting) to learn to shepherd from the front of the flock if you can. Today, workers are more educated and connected than before. They won't follow blindly and they will question. Beating butts with a stick is exhausting and will turn the flock skittish, paranoid, maybe even vorpal. Getting them to voluntarily follow you, ah, now there's the trick!

Shepherding from the front means knowing a little about what is ahead. Daily happenings can distract us from larger trends. A good follower keeps half of his or her attention focused beyond the car in front of them. Think about it: would a racecar driver fiddle with a radio dial or text a message at 250 miles an hour in a steep curve? Maybe, but at that moment you can bet that almost all of that driver's attention is focused outside of the car.

Franklin Roosevelt, a genius at picking and persuading the right people to set up innovative programs like the Civilian Conservation Corps and Social Security, said, "A good leader can't get too far ahead of his followers." True enough, but that implies a responsibility on the part of managers and followers to keep up.

Tenet 16
Courtesy is a basic human responsibility

I've seen leaders make secretaries cry. I've seen spouses of those same secretaries become the leader's boss. There is justice and it ain't always pretty. Surviving in any organization is like living in a small town: you never really know who's related to the mayor or his mistress so praise publicly and criticize in private. And only do either when you can do it constructively.

Courtesy is about being nice, but in this context it is also about respecting the boundaries of chosen roles. Just as you might choose to follow, the leader has chosen to lead. Each role deserves a little courteous respect.

A whole separate tenet could and probably should be written about followership in marriages and relationships. As perhaps the most complicated and intimate of leadership/followership interactions, an emphasis on courtesy in that context can be both a tell for the relationship's success and a clue to its role as a catalyst.

Tenet 17
Additive vs. subtractive

As a follower, it's important to determine if the leader you follow is subtractive or additive. In art, there are two types of creative processes: additive creativity and subtractive. A sculptor, for example, can add to a block of clay, or a painter collage-up a canvas until it's the size of a house and still have room to add to it. She's just limited by time and resources. A carver, on the other hand, works with a finite piece of lumber and had better achieve his intended masterpiece before he runs out of wood. It's the same for leaders. An additive leader is only limited by the amount of time and resources they continue to bring to their vision. A subtractive leader is limited by the math: 1-1= nothing.

If you're following an additive leader, don't worry so much about what the end state is going to look like. That's not your lot, nor your responsibility. Besides, an additive leader may change even that towards the end. Your main job is to hold the tools, bring more material and pile it on wherever you're told.

If you're following a subtractive leader, you should be very attuned to the end state because the time to get there, the amount o fmaterial that needs to be removed, is finite. Potentially as one of those numbers in the equation, your removal might be or become a subtracted element in the final outcome.

Now, this is mostly just analogy and yes, there are exceptions. What if, for example, your leader's job is to build a cave? The more she removes the more she's successful. Yes, there are exceptions. I'm just saying, as a good follower, pay attention.

Tenet 18
Connect

Picture yourself as a fly face down in a glass of water. It's filled almost to the very top and your only hope is to drink or you will drown. Do, or die. Just go with me on this one. Impossible? Yes, if you have to do it alone but what if it was you and a million other thirsty flies?

Now forget the other flies. Picture your leader as an ant on your back.
If you drown, she drowns, too, but since she's sitting a little taller in the water
than you, she can see just over the rim that more flies are coming. Maybe
she can call on the Ant Patrol to bring a stick. The point is, at that moment in
time, she needs you and since she has access to more info (and you really don't
have any other options), you need her, too. A follower's success or failure lies
in the relationships, both with the ant and a million flies.

Tenet 19
Know the Triggers

To expand on Tenet 17's point to pay attention, every great follower
learns their leader's trigger points, and their own. I'm not talking about lines
the leader won't cross, although knowing those is another trait of a great
follower.

By trigger points I mean the not-so-trivial process-influencers
that concern, frighten, or sometimes even panic, a leader. Leaders—and
great followers—have created maps in their head that lead from "here" to
"successful outcome." The map has already identified where the barriers are
likely to be, where bridges have to be built, how far the leader will have to
take their subordinates, and how much time it will take. People wandering off
the trail, unseen beasties threatening from the bushes, or anything that affects a
leader's ability to get to "success" pulls a trigger.

Every leader has these idiosyncrasies and they are different in every
leader. One trigger might be suddenly not having enough time to get the job

done right. Another, perhaps, is not being heard, or worse, being ignored. Whatever it is, a great follower learns to anticipate these and either minimizes (as best they can) the events that set off these triggers or mitigates the consequences of the bullets for their peers and subordinates in the line of fire.

Knowing what lines the leader won't cross is key, too. It's those issues that cause her to take an intransigent stand, or otherwise evokes in him the figurative action of drawing a line in the sand with the organizational flag, planting it decisively in the ground, and loudly declaring "this far and no more." Sometimes decrees like this are warranted, but once declared they can be hard for most leaders to retract and any absolute limits options. An anticipating follower can tactfully suggest compromises or alternatives in advance, or at the very least whisper "Do you really want to . . . ?" consequence questions in the boss's ear.

Tenet 20
Look for the Fear

One of the triggers is so ever-present that it deserves to be recognized as its own tenet: fear.

For the follower, fear may be about change or loss of control. It might be something more tangible and literal: fear for life or limb, or the life and limbs of a co-follower or family. A leader may fear their subordinates won't follow, or that they can't fulfil the mission that they've been given. Leaders may fear not having the resources they need to accomplish the milestones or to move the barriers.

Fear can manifest itself as defensive behavior in followers: hesitancy, anger, absence, just to mention a few signs among thousands. In leaders, it's often seen as offensive (vs. defensive, not as in "bad"). Sure, in its most overt or extreme cases, it might be the cause of bullying or intimidation, but it also might be a trigger for something productive and positive. Fear may ramp up the timetable to reach a goal, for example.

Ultimately, a great follower's goal is to enable their leader's success, so identifying the presence and sources of fear and fear's consequences is critical. That said, however, it's just bad form, unnecessary, and often unproductive for a great follower to be the cause of it. Fear is caustic and like anything corrosive, its nature breaks things down. While a little fear may dissolve some gunk in the gears, a lot will eventually eat away the gear shaft. And nobody wants that. A great follower is looking to make their leader successful, yes, but they are also the catalyst that encourages the rank-and-file to march on. And in the long run fear has its limits. Over time, courtesy, respect, wisdom and knowledge, and the like may be more useful tools in a great follower's Batman Utility Belt.

Tenet 21
Feedback has power

A leader is like a farmer on a mule cart. Up high, one hand on the brake, he's in control, right? If following was only about being the mule, that might be true, but it's not. Good followership also is about being the reins, the footboard, and yes, sometimes the bench seat. Reins, footboards and seats give the farmer the feedback she needs to steer the cart. Change the feedback and

you can influence the cart's speed and direction, maybe help keep it out of the ditch.

Predictability builds trust with leaders, but not necessarily the way you may think it does. If you're predictably evil, or let's say a poor performer, leaders will give you responsibilities and trust you only up to the level of your competence, knowing they can predict and control the outcome. Spontaneity or random acts of productive, kind, or otherwise beneficial behaviors may build distrust, not necessarily in you, the follower, but in a predictable system.

Beware of the leader who asks, "How'm I doing?" I can remember three times in my working career that I've had top brass ask me that question. Once it was at a senior board meeting; once on an executive plane with my entire chain of supervision aboard; and once I was asked the question with all my team and coworkers present.

If the leader asks for your feedback in a public setting, especially with your peers or supervisors around, they're probably fishing for validation. If they ask it one-on-one, a good follower owes them the courtesy of an honest answer. For one thing, it may be your only chance to affect real change but think through your answer in advance. How well do you know and trust your leader? Is the question genuine or patronizing? What's the likelihood that the leader will act on your comments? Could your advice adversely affect your peers or subordinates?

Tenet 22
Think it through...all the way

A corollary to "Don't do as you're told" is "Think," or maybe "Don't die for stupid causes." You may want to take this advice figuratively but I almost really do mean it literally. Don't die stupidly for causes and don't die for stupid causes. To blindly follow a leader into a dark rabbit hole is a Darwin moment. If a stupid leader dies with a stupid follower, it kind of stays in balance, but if a stupid leader survives the rabbit hole, well, now there's one more person generating stupid ideas than there are to carry them out.

Lieutenant Colonel (and former general) George Custer lost the lives of more than 200 soldiers and highly decorated and experienced officers at Little Bighorn. Field Marshall John French and Sir Ian Hamilton, just two of the authors of World War I military strategies, caused the loss of millions of lives. General Maurice Gamelin drew a line in the sand with a string of "impenetrable" forts across northern France that the German Army almost literally jumped over to start WWII.

History is full of examples of people blindly following leaders stupidly or for stupid causes. In a year, in ten years, they're just as dead and their causes or sacrifices forgotten. Through blind obedience, ignorance, suspension of analytical thought, or whatever, they've VOLUNTARILY clipped their own bud off of the evolutionary, the Darwin, tree.

Tenet 23
Don't fear the shadows

By definition leadership has to have followers, and by definition leadership leads and followers follow. To be most efficient, expedient, and effective, an organization's leaders push for uniformity: everyone follows the same goals, the same rules. Everyone makes the same moves at the same time. Leadership's inner circle is really a group of apostles, following an appointed, or sometimes self-appointed, guru. The guru comes up with these rules and the inner circle institutionalizes and enforces them.

If you are one of the apostles, it's too late for you to make change. You're stuck with the rulebook. If you don't follow it, you won't continue to be an apostle. In a sense, the rules, the goals, the moves are leading YOU. If you're not one of the appointed ones but care enough about the mission to want to affect change, you have to be ahead of the game unfolding on the board. The players on the board are confined by the rules of the game: they follow procedures, get permissions, find funding, etc. But an unseen game changer may be running around the board's edges to get to the right spot ahead of everyone else. A game changer might be working off the board completely, perhaps floating over players through personal influence with a stakeholder or under game pieces by greasing certain sticking points so that they move easier than others. The game changer may be working on a different timetable altogether, their actions unrecognized or incomprehensible to others, quietly beating away at one small spot in the dike long enough to create a flood over time.

Every organization has these people. If leadership doesn't know that, they're left scratching their heads wondering why some things seem to work while other things don't. Leadership can get paranoid about what they can't see or affect, so once they see the shadows moving around the board or cogs that seem to turn themselves, it's natural to want to excise those things from the game.

But leaders and good followers don't have to surgically remove what they don't understand. The secret is first to know to look for game changers and then second, once spotted, try to understand each game changer's motivation. Are they for or against the organization? If their actions enable the organization to be successful, let them do their thing. Maybe even (gasp!) enable them.

Tenet 24
Good leaders aren't wise ones

Well, some are, but it's lagniappe.

Wisdom requires insights into multiple points of view and a wise person looks for common ground and compromise. A wise person has empathy in spades and good followers have that AND the drive to sacrifice a part of themselves—by giving their time or subservience, perhaps—to make sure their leaders succeed.

In place of wisdom, good leaders possess equally important skills, among them strong communication, persuasion, and logic. That leader is a leader because he or she has demonstrated a drive to achieve a goal, and such drive requires focus and exclusion: focus of attention, resources and time, and exclusions of distractions, lesser goals, and wastes of time. For a focused leader, other people's goals and visions are wastes-of-time distractions. Like pressure on one side of a fulcrum, a good leader applies force on one side to move the lever with deliberate speed, force and direction. A wise person, on the other hand, is looking for balance, finding compromises across the lever for an optimal stable state. There are always exceptions, of course, and GREAT leaders will have or will know to develop wisdom, too.

Respect the person you've chosen to follow, but always keep your integrity and remember Tenet #21. A good follower will know not to expect leadership to be wise. A great follower will anticipate lapses in wisdom, prepare for them, and fill in or try to compensate for those lapses when they can. And since good leaders aren't necessarily wise but need wise advisers, guess what? Tag, you're it!

Tenet 25
Leaders, managers and followers

In 2014, when the Ebola virus broke out in Sierra Leone, the World Health Organization's strategy to find sick people included sending volunteers with mobile phones into the local chiefdoms to trace contacts and then alert the Ministry of Health if they found any suspicious cases or deaths. Sierra Leone's Chief Medical Officer, Dr. Brima Kargbo, team leaders and emergency coordinators organized roughly 300 volunteers. In this example, it might be hard to tell who was leading, managing, and following. Was Kargbo a manager of the WHO effort or was he the key local leader at Ground Zero? Would someone stepping forward voluntarily to enter a potentially deadly environment be considered a leader? Or because they were on the very tail end of a worldwide health emergency, were they one of the followers? Perhaps because those volunteers were willing to take such risks, they fall into the category of "#1#2," a great follower?

Being a leader and being in a leadership position aren't necessarily the same things. Some Presidents of the United States were just good managers; some very talented leaders get "stuck" in manager roles. What defines each isn't their title or assigned station. It is their go-to approach to problem solving: motivate, organize, or facilitate.

A good leader sees the blissful beach on the other side of the mountain and convinces everyone to go there. A good manager makes sure the mountain path is clear, that the supplies are stocked for the journey, and that everyone stays tied together on the way. Good followers make sure they are personally in shape, that their gloves and Band-Aids are handy, and that they are wearing adequate boots. A GREAT follower stays in shape, wears their gloves, boots and Band-Aids, AND makes sure to pack floaties, flip-flops and sunscreen, enough to share when everyone gets to that beach.

Tenet 26
The delegation paradox

A great follower is usually given -- or voluntarily takes on -- more and more responsibilities. Competence is usually rewarded with more work but one person can't do it all, so a great follower will learn to delegate. And every task delegated requires some form of convincing and follow-up and consequences have to be levied if the delegated task isn't delivered on-quality or on-time. Convincing, follow-up, consequences: they're all leadership actions. In short, does successfully delegating a task now define you as a leader, instead of "just" a good follower?

To make the Allies Operation Overload, or D-Day, plan succeed during the Second World War, Supreme Headquarters commander General Dwight Eisenhower and General Bernard Montgomery, commander of the 21st Army Group, needed to convince 156,000 United States, British, and Canadian soldiers to take back five beaches from the German Army along 50-miles of north French coastline. Each beach had a code name. From west to east they were Utah and Omaha, assigned to the Americans; Gold, to British forces; Juno, a Canadian objective; and Sword, also assigned to the British. The beaches were heavily fortified and the Germans were expecting some form of attack along the coast: they just didn't know exactly when or from where it would come.

If convincing men to bravely face German resistance wasn't already a nearly-impossible task, the operation required incredibly-detailed planning;

months of secret training; and a long logistical chain to support the actual invasion day and the months to follow. Overlord coordinated the movements of more than 5,000 ships and 11,000 aircraft. Many an offensive during that war and the war before, WWI, had run fast and far, only to lose momentum when complicated re-staffing and resupply plans ran dry or were cut to pieces by the enemy. For Overlord to succeed, planners had to account for a subsequent push up and over the cliffs and into the coastal villages. Simultaneously, without knowing the final disposition (or positions, for that matter) of Operation Overload troops, teams worked tirelessly to lay the foundations of reliable transportation, communication, and supply support networks for an invading, offensive force that could cross France east to Berlin.

Of course, General Eisenhower delegated to other leaders the tasks of landing on the five beaches, preparing for D-Day, and establishing support to the troops. For example, Lieutenant General Gerard Bucknall, British 30th Corps, with its 50th Infantry Division led by Major General Douglas Graham, were assigned to take Gold Beach. British Lieutenant General John Crocker was delegated responsibility to secure Sword. On Utah Beach, Major General J. Lawton Collin's 7th Army and the 8th, 22nd, and 12th infantry regiments of the U.S.'s 4th Infantry Division led by Major General Raymond O. Barton were asked to establish a beachhead to land supplies and begin coordinating support to the 82nd and 101st American airborne divisions. At lower levels, other leaders were orchestrating their assignments. Brig. General Theodore Roosevelt Jr., the eldest son of U.S. President Theodore Roosevelt (no pressure there!), landed in Utah Beach's first assault wave. Brig. General Don Forrester Pratt, assistant division commander for the U.S.'s 101st Airborne Division, landed in the first wave of

gliders two miles west of Utah's objective, Sainte-Marie-du-Mont. General Pratt never made it alive off of the landing field; Roosevelt Jr. died in France a month later.

The point? From top down and at every level of execution, no one can deny that Operation Overlord was led by brave soldiers, mariners, and airmen. Each a selfless leader; each a follower (even Eisenhower), who was delegated a task to do. Even followers must delegate but in the absence of the authority given to or assumed by leaders, such followers must use every skill they have or have learned from their leader to accomplish their assignment.

Yes, delegating is hard. It's risky, a risk that run-of-the-mill followers aren't willing to take. Arguably, it is the single, defining trait that, once employed successfully, sets a great follower on the path (gasp!) of becoming a leader. Delegating requires good judgement about the character of those delegated to. It demands a wise understanding of both the task's details and its ultimate objective. It requires trust of other followers and those followers' trust of you, all of which is built before the task must be assigned. Delegating to another follower implies an authority and a penalty for failure, neither of which a great follower has the means to inflict.

Does that make a follower a leader or just a leader-in-sheep's-clothing? Does it really matter?

Tenet 27
Taking criticism: grace under fire

Ninety-nine percent of the time, a great follower's contribution to the success of a leader's idea is in the quality of its execution, not the idea itself or its revolutionary or innovative conception.

Virginia Katherine McMath was born in 1911 in Independence, Missouri. Raised by her grandparents, Virginia eventually joined her mother and stepfather in Dallas, where, to everyone's surprise at age 15 she won a Charleston dance contest and landed a four-week dance contract traveling around the country. With her mother at her side to guide her, Virginia picked up stage experience in vaudeville and eventually began an acting career in films and on Broadway. By then, of course, she was already going by her nickname, Ginger, and had adopted her step-father's last name, Rogers.

A few years after playing bit parts in minor movies, the public took serious notice of Ginger's talents when she sang and danced her way through two movies, The Gold Diggers of 1933, and 42nd Street. But when she was paired that same year with a young dancer named Fred Astaire in RKO's "Flying Down to Rio," the two became an instant sensation. It was said later that he gave her class and she gave him sex appeal. In truth, Astaire was a dancer and singer who could act; Rogers was an actress who could also dance.

At first, Astaire said of Rogers, "I did not go into pictures to be teamed with her or anyone else and if that is the program in mind for me I will not stand for it. I'd rather not make any more pictures for Radio [RKO] if I have to be teamed up with one of those 'movie queens." Astaire was certainly qualified to criticize. He'd started dancing with his sister on Broadway when he as four years old and he became a master at creating entertaining dance numbers. But he demanded perfection; each retake a criticism in itself. In her book "Ginger, My Story," Rogers recalled her feet bleeding after rehearsals. She wrote that if he got an idea for a new dance routine, it wasn't unusual for him to call her any time day or night to explain it and convince her to show up very early the next morning to rehearse it. A great follower, Ginger Rogers was required to match every step Fred did, but anticipate his moves, do them all backwards, gracefully, flawlessly, and in high heels.*

First appearing in a Frank & Ernest comic strip by cartoonist Bob Thaves in 1982 but made popular by politician and Ronald Reagan-staffer Faith Whittlesey at a White House speech in 1984.

Yet, Fred always seems to get full credit for coming up with the dance steps and for effortlessly leading his partner across movie sets and stages. It's Fred, not Ginger, who's widely considered the greatest popular-music dancer of all time. In her book, Rogers relates some of her more memorable contributions to the couple's routines, such as suggesting the endings in the duet's Top Hat and Carefree numbers; dancing on roller skates in Shall We Dance; and the pair's hypnotizing moves in Carefree.

The duo became Hollywood legends, performing together in ten films. They remain among the movie industry's star elite, remembered to this day as "Fred and Ginger," although Rogers completed 63 other films and earned an Academy Award for Best Actress on her own.

C.S. Lewis once wrote "I contend that when your own work is being criticized you are, in one sense, in an especially advantageous position for detecting the goodness or badness of the critique." More qualified than anyone to comment on Fred as the pair's lead and ever the enabling, great follower, Rogers graciously said of Astaire, "I loved Fred so, and I mean that in the nicest, warmest way: I had such affection for him artistically. I think that experience with Fred was a divine blessing. It blessed me, I know, and I don't think blessings are one sided." *("Ginger: Salute to a Star," Dick Richards, London Sunday Times Magazine)*

C.S. Lewis went on to write "Ignorant as he may be about his books value, [the author] is at least an expert on its content." (C.S. Lewis, On stories, Harvest/HBJ Books, 1966). Likewise, while leaders might criticize the results of their plan's objectives, a Great Folllower is usually the expert in executing the plan's details.

This point about criticism is better made using a more contemporary example. After Stephen King won the National Book Award's prestigious Medal for Distinguished Contribution to American Letters, Yale professor and literary critic Harold Bloom wasn't impressed. Said Bloom, "[King] is a man who writes what used to be called 'penny dreadfuls.' That [the judges] could believe that there is any literary value there or any aesthetic accomplishment or signs of an inventive human intelligence is simply a testimony to their own idiocy."

Whether or not you read or like Stephen King's works, there's no denying he knows better than anyone both his genre of terror AND his trade as a writer. In the nearly 50 years since his first book, Carrie, King has authored more than 50 novels, all circulated world-wide. His first crime novel won the Edgar Award for best novel and he received the National Medal of Arts in 2014. Now in his mid-70s, King's net worth is estimated at a half billion dollars.

King didn't invent the suspenseful story, he just took its execution – pun intended – to the level of a new art form. Rogers may not have been the inventive genius behind Astaire's dance routines, but there's no denying those routines were elevated to "Unforgettable!" when SHE was the partner swinging on the end of his arms.

What would American popular culture look like today if Ginger or

Stephen had stopped being Ginger or Stephen because of the criticism they'd received? How much would the luster, the quality, of American cinema and literature have been tarnished? Would we even give their respective genres a second look if they hadn't reset the bar so high? Similarly, how much might be lost whenever a great follower shrinks like a touch-me-not plant under the criticism – justified or not -- of their leader?

Tenet 28
Flair vs. flamboyance

Tenet Four, "Do the right thing…quietly" doesn't really address the fact that a Great Follower has to be enabled to get things done, if not by their leader, then at least by those the follower must convince. Obviously, this means that first, the follower must get noticed and develop some relevance.

A great follower will be seen as "having a flair" for things, or someone who "just knows how things work," or who has been "around long enough to get things done." Few can be as effective if they're perceived to be flamboyant, ostentatious, self-indulgent, or worse, self-serving, a know-it-all, past their usefulness, or irrelevant.

It's one thing to execute with elegant style, and quite another to overbuild or add costly and unnecessary features just to get more attention.

Rococco, a short-lived art movement in the early 1700s, was an outgrowth of a bored nobility, excised from the Versaille countryside after Louis XIV's death. Cast from their pastoral retreats, these French socialites found themselves attempting to redecorate new homes in Paris. Known for its light themes, playful colors, and frivolous, purposeless ornamentation, Rococco was a reflection of a nearly frivolous, purposeless noble class, a class soon to be caught and shaken like a rabbit by a pit bull called the French Revolution.

You'll recall from your Art 101 class that the Renaissance was influenced by the simultaneous emergence of scientific study. Similarly, Neo-classicism ideals developed with the late 18th Century Age of Enlightenment. Just as scientific thought and observation supplanted outdated Medieval conventions during the Renaissance, the social movement towards efficiency and class equality in Neo-classical themes rendered Rococco irrelevant a couple of centuries later.

It pays to be recognized as the follower with a little (or a lot) of Renaissance flair, but not so much that you're seen as flamboyant Rococco. There is an art to becoming important enough to be valued and held above the crowd, but not ostentatious enough to be noticed and targeted by those three percent mentioned in Tenet 8.

Tenet 29
Don't panic early

First as NASA's liaison to Space Camp in Huntsville, Ala, in the mid-2000s, then as the director of strategic planning for a medium-sized science museum near New Orleans in the 2010s, I had the opportunity to work with a number of national figures and influential community leaders who served on Boards of Directors. I had the privilege of observing their leadership styles.

Boards of Directors are an interesting mix of leaders and followers. While some are legacy figureheads, most Board members are invited to be board members because they bring something to the (conference room) table. For most, it's funding or the ability to find some. Many are asked to serve on a board because they possess a honed skill. Maybe it's investing, accounting, or possessing corporate history. For a select few, it's their eminence, their renown. But across your board tenure, if you're lucky, there's that one, quiet member sitting somewhere in the middle of the room who has become the group's bedrock of humanism. Maybe he or she is a living example of perseverance; or it's their emotional investment to the cause; or a commitment of time, values, or compassion, but this one person sets the tone of the board, and thus, for the entire organization.

One such board member I came to greatly appreciate and admire was Apollo 13 astronaut Fred Haise. A delightful human being, engineer, philosopher, and tireless advocate for all things science, space, and engineering, Fred is not only a central character in NASA's "most successful failure," the aborted Apollo 13 moon landing mission, but a test pilot survivor of four aircraft accidents, commander of four early Shuttle test flights, and the CEO of a successful division of Grumman Aerospace. Fred's personal mantra: "Don't Panic Early" became the unofficial mantra of the senior staff of our young science museum as we struggled in the early years to keep it financially afloat.

Tenet 30
Panic envy

A corollary to Astronaut Fred Haise's personal mantra, "Don't Panic

Early," is the followership mantra, "Panic Envy," or more to the point, "Panic Empathy." If the leader you've chosen to follow suddenly panics because of the overwhelming responsibilities he or she has undertaken, remember that as the leader, the consequences of leadership are their responsibilities to shoulder, not yours.

Your task as a Great Follower is to help your leader get over and past the panic so they can continue with their more strategic vision: so they can continue to lead. How each Great Follower does that can be a beauty to watch; a dance of rhetoric, humor, or small, enabling actions that break up the panic into palatable, smaller bites. It's not necessarily about avoiding the

panic meal altogether: it can be more about helping a leader swallow the panic and then get up from the table and back to work.

Tenet 31
Causible deniability

It's important to make decisions on the right causes in cause-verses-effect relationships. The causality will influence your next decision, and the ones after that. If an underlining cause is wrong, it can skew what follows.

Say that you covered up a basketball with a blanket, then piled 20 bed sheets on top of the bump. You'd notice that the bump from the ball gets bigger and bigger the more you pile sheets and blankets on top of it. If you don't happen to have a basketball around, draw a dot in the middle of the bottom of a piece of paper, then draw a line from the left margin to the dot, over and around it, then continue the line to the other side of the page. Now, draw a line above the first, following the contoured bump around the dot but always staying parallel to the first line. Then draw another line, and another, and another. You'll notice that the bump just gets bigger and bigger, a magnification of its cause.

As another way of illustrating the point, picture a drug your doctor gives you for diabetes. You're told to cut out all carbohydrates and you're supposed to take this drug for three months, and then you and your doctor will reassess your treatment. YOU think your drug is designed to directly work on your insulin, physically reducing the levels your pancreas secretes. But the drug is actually

designed to make you very nauseous when it comes in contact with carbs so that if you dive into a plate of French fries or binge on a box of doughnuts, you (and your body) will regret it soon afterwards. The drug is really designed to change your behavior. Now the doctor won't tell you this because, after all, who but the most strong-willed or strongly motivated new diabetic would voluntarily take such a medication, especially after the first few episodes of cramps, muscle spasms, vomiting, and "the squits?" Assuming you stay the course and complete your three-month drug regiment, the result – lower AIC numbers – is the same: you've reached your A1C goal.

Your assumption, however, that the cause of change comes from altered levels of pancreas secretion, although supported by your own observations, is plausible, but false. Your new normal really comes from changes in your eating habits. Does knowing the truth change your ideas about how you make assumptions? About your doctor or pharmaceuticals? Or when to plan for potty breaks when you're at work, traveling, or shopping?

So, as to be unambiguous: it's important to understand the real reasons behind actions. If you're going to decide (and delegate) work, a great follower needs to deeply understand the mechanics of the task and not assume that just because they saw a process work once, it will automatically provide the same results a second time, even if they're drawing from personally-observed experience. Unfortunately, a nearly endless list of invisible things can cause the squits.

Tenet 32
Be all in...but

Although at some point you may decide you can no longer follow your leader, while you are following him or her, be all in…BUT…

It only takes a glimpse at film clips of Adolph Hitler's rallies from Nuremberg, Germany, in the late 1930s and early 40s, before questioning followers (or self-aware leaders) must ask themselves "Why would somebody choose to follow something so obviously evil?"

Put aside the part of the answer that starts with "Hindsight is always

20/20," and focus on the charisma of the leader and the mindset of the faithful follower. Psychanalyst Erich Fromm in 1941 suggested that in Hitler's and Germany's case such a relationship developed out of a kind of sickness in the German culture at the time, a sado-masochistic psychosis, possibly a remnant of the loss of identity after the First World War, that polarized and energized dominance and submissive behaviors towards authority ("The Other Authoritarian Personality, Bob Altemeyer, Univ. of Manitoba, Winnipeg, Political Psychology, 1988, pg 84).

Fromm's theory was given some weight during the now-famous Berkeley research experiments published by Adorno, Frenkel-Brunswik, Levinson, & Sanford in 1950. The experiment asked subjects to send electrical shocks to patients to keep the patients in line for their own good. Prompted by an authority figure to administer more and more severe shocks to (non-existent) patients, subjects in the experiments helped the researchers identify an "authoritarian submission" personality trait, an extreme behavior of fascist-minded personalities to both submit and dominate. A book about leadership might question the motivations of the experiment's authoritarians. Fortunately for us, in the decade or two that followed the Berkeley experiments, related research tended to focus on the reactions of the subject – the followers -- to such authority and scientists have identified clues to some very interesting followership tenets.

For one thing, researchers created a "Right-Wing Authoritarianism," or RWA, scale (Altemeyer, 1981, 1988, 1996) that measured and rated authoritarian personalities on how strongly they believed in submission to authority and how aggressive and appropriate a measure should be applied to achieve it. Thought to develop in childhood as a response to obedience, conventionalism, and aggression, the trait tends to manifest itself in adulthood in ethnocentric (ie. "my norms matter") attitudes and consensual validation ("I'm gonna hang with people just like me") behaviors. RWA thinking is rooted more in memorization of what persons of perceived higher authority have told them than on their own critical, independent experiences or appraisals. RWA personalities also show a tendency to want to defend a pecking order of power as a way of preserving their place in line, putting down those perceived as weaker or more vulnerable. At the extreme end of the scale, RWAs don't recognize their own contradictions, advocating for Americanism, for example, while ignoring the concept of "justice and liberty for all." Some studies also indicate a trend towards sexual assault of women among high-level RWA men (Walker, Rowe, Quinsey, 1993). They could be classified as scared. They see the world as dangerous; they self-identify as "moral;" and they are conservative in the sense that they are averse to any change that threatens their beliefs or their place in the order of things.

In another study, researchers were able to establish a scale to measure social dominance orientation (SDO). In a series of 12 student studies (Pratto, Sidanius, and Malle, 1994), researchers were able to indicate and predict correlations between a person's attitudes towards equal vs. hierarchial intergroup relationships and their attitudes towards concepts such as nationalism, cultural elitism, patriotism, and racism.

Then in 1996, in a limited study since reproduced with similar results, researchers compiled abbreviated versions of 18 personality tests, including the RWA and SDO scales, looking for a correlation between personality types and the above attitudes -- prejudice, patriotism, etc. (McFarland and Aderlson, 1996). Their findings confirmed a strong connection between these attitudes and social dominator and right-wing authoritarian personalities. Furthermore, later studies have determined that such social authoritarian attitudes towards groups correlate with interpersonal attitudes as well. That's not to say that high-ranked RWAs and SDOs believe the same thing -- they might or might not -- only that their approach towards authority in society closely corresponds to how they approach one-on-one relationships.

What's all this have to do with Followership? Well, look at the leader you choose to follow and at their one-on-one relationships with their deputies, spouses, friends, and peers. Applied, research would indicate that their attitudes towards the people they personally come in contact with every day is indeed linked to their beliefs about how society in general should behave and how its subgroups should be treated. In other words, to the extent a leader believes authority should be forced both up and down the perceived power ladder is a factor that drives their decision-making process, their ethics, their rationalization, hiring decisions, and strategic direction choices.

Tenet 33
Recognize extremism

A study started by the Norwegian Police Academy College in 1997, the Exit Norway Project, has produced some interesting and counter-intuitive insights into what entices a potential follower to join extremist groups or follow extreme philosophies. As it turns out, the root attraction isn't the philosophy itself but the need to be accepted into a group. Extremist groups just happen to provide a path of least resistance, lowering the bar for acceptance into their group to just one notch above the floor: "hate as we hate and you're in." Then, such groups have a patent formula for grooming their recruits into action. That formula includes three strategies.

Before continuing, it's important to point out what might be obvious to most people: the term "extremist" is a relative point on a gamut line that runs in two directions, with "universally socially acceptable" as its mid-point. The gamut line itself might be religious, political, a lifestyle, race, or something else entirely.

The first element in the extremists' formula requires the initiate to discard alternative explanations. The follower is presented only black-and-white arguments. In other words, every argument is polarized into an either/or think set. Gone are life's gray areas, the "maybes" and exceptions. "Either you're for us or against us; if it's this way, it's always this way; this is right because we're always right."

Secondly, the leaders' claim that members of their group are superior to everything and everyone else.

And lastly, the follower is taught to see all dissenters and targets of hate in derogatory terms. "We're good and they are bad; in a black-or-white world, we are very good and they happen to be very, very bad." Leaders of extreme groups give their targets of hate such "lesser" animalistic labels, such as "rats," "parasites," or "vermin that need to be exterminated."

This is the first step towards galvanizing a new recruit to act out, legitimizing the risk and consequences of any future action they should decide or be told to take on behalf of the group that has so openly accepted them. After all, such extremist groups claim, "our" group is so superior that it knows all the world's underlying truths and what's best. They are convinced – and attempt to convince the extremist follower – that not only are their arguments the only right way, but, being superior, "you are part of THE elite" group privy to insights no one else can possess. Eventually, they argue, all the inferior rest will see that they are inferior and "we" will rule/replace/lead/conquer/prevail over them.

The Exit Norway Project suggest that the way to disengage an extremist follower is to remove the extremist philosophy from the follower's head AND physically remove the follower from the social group. Then, both the philosophy and the socialization voids need to be filled with something else. For many people, rational thinking, science, or interpersonal exposure can become the scaffolding for a new philosophy. Some join military, church, or social service circles.   (Simon Copland, in the May 1 2019 BBC article "How do you prevent extremism")

Tenet 34
Know the state you're in

As a corollary to both Tenet 19, "Know the Triggers" and Tenet 24,

"Good Leaders Aren't Wise Ones," another tenet about motivations is "Know the state you're in" because when you commit to support a leader, you're in THEIR shadow, affected by their state of mind, even their time of life.

It's worth keeping tabs on the ecosystem surrounding your leader's motivations. "Surrounding," though, is almost an inaccurate word in this context since it can imply inward-facing forces in a two-dimensional plane, like a circle surrounding a dot. A better term might be "encompassing," which describes something in three-dimensions and forces applied from above and below as well as all around.

One red flag that demands you take a closer look at your leader's state of life or state of mind is when they throw a tantrum. We've all seen it, the boss's equivalent to road rage. Call it commander dander, or the tantrum itself a "dom bomb" or "pilotage hemorrhage." Not unlike a road rage, maybe your office refers to them simply as boss hissy-fits.

Unlike office hissy fits, however, according to an article in Psychiatry Magazine (June, 2010), road rage is now recognized as a legitimate disorder. It's described as "a constellation of thoughts, emotions, ad behaviors that occur in response to a perceived unjustified provocation." Sometimes it's exacerbated by alcohol or drug abuse, but not always, and typically its offenders tend to be immature or young males. While most road rage episodes manifest in only boisterous shouting and gesturing, about two percent escalate to direct and damaging contact. Episodes can be brought on by a number of environmental factors (like needing to perform a high number of tasks in quick succession, for example, or a demand or perceived need to travel more or faster), or psychological factors, such as displaced aggressions or the attribution of blame onto others). Sound familiar?

These tantrums aside, other behaviors and states of mind might include:

<u>Deer-in-the-headlights syndrome</u>: characterized by paralysis usually brought on by a recent episode of punishment or severe lacerations from above.

<u>The Up-and-Coming</u> or <u>Something to Prove</u> stages: often characterized by change, sometimes little-understood chaos, challenges to paradigms, and new norms. A nimble follower may find this time in a leader's work life exhilarating but even highly-experienced followers may need to hone their communication and persuasion skills to avoid "rework frustration." This leadership behavior should not be confused with a leader's State of Hail Mary Passes, which can be identified by a series of high risk-taking endeavors, usually accompanied by short, intense adrenalin rushes, not always positive.

<u>The Building Stage</u> (ie: of a team, personal empire, processes, etc.): Given adequate time and good support from their followers, leaders sometimes can find themselves in a state where everything and everyone seems to be clicking along in unison. When problems arise, they're quickly and adequately handled; goals are reached in reasonable time; and "the Plan" is moving forward to its predictable conclusion. Often recognized by its uncharacteristic praise and recognition of subordinates, this stage is an especially dangerous time for Great Followers, who can become exposed by success. While tempted to relax their guard, Great Followers must

none-the-less regularly inspect the tracks and look in front of the engine to anticipate inevitable roadblocks.

The Already Arrived or Nearly Departed: The former is an optimal state of mind, one that makes a follower's ability to serve so much easier. The latter, arguably the worst stage for a good leader, can challenge even the most stalwart follower to perform during episodes of their leader's regret, malaise, distraction, or lack of focus on longer-term issues.

Dead Man Walking: Sometimes a leader's leader has pulled all support, effectively neutering your boss's ability to affect change, enable progress, or put resources to his or her initiatives. Often this is NOT a statement about a leader's leadership qualities but it does point to their dulled effectiveness. This is when a leader still worth following benefits from a follower's ability to work in the dark shadows, manage invisible connections, and apply all the salves and tonics in his or her med bag to mend the wound as best they can. Great Followers won't even leave a scar!

Perhaps you've experienced other states of mind or states of life, but while you're noticing a leader's state of life, take some time to examine of your own. You can be sure that those who you'll ask to follow with you certainly are.

Tenet 35
The magic mirror

Tenet 34 is a corollary to other tenets but this one is a corollary to Tenet 34,

"Know the State You're In."

Like the Mirror-on-the-Wall in the Snow White fairy tale, sometimes you can be asked questions by people in leadership positions. It's hard to answer such questions productively without some hints about its context. Why are you asking? Why now? Why are you asking ME?

Before answering, you should already be at least vaguely aware of the broader context of a leader's stage in life. After all, leaders are people too, with family problems, midlife crises, money problems, etc. You should also understand the risks and benefits you face in your answer to Mirror, Mirror on the Wall questions. Is the question really the question or is it an analogy or allegory of the real problem the leader is struggling with? Are you being asked for "feedback," "advice," "consultation," or validation? If the answer isn't something you think leadership is going to want to hear, what's the best way to tactfully, but clearly, answer the question?

In my working career, I slowly progressed from junior officer and account manager, to senior officer and technical expert. Never given full decision-making or course-setting special powers, I've served as an advisor to the Board of Directors; as a paid, contracted-for expert, and even served as a strategic direct-report to the CEO. All follower positions; all positions that demanded I accept the responsibility to provide my leader with valuable feedback, asked for or not.

When I was younger or considered to be less experienced, more times than not I was asked for feedback by a leader genuinely looking for a fresh perspective. There was no ego involved: the leader, after all, was older and wiser, and could quickly disregard anything he or she didn't want to hear because that "nice young man just doesn't understand the bigger picture." Tactlessness or a lack of finesse when answering my leader at that stage was forgivable, almost cute.

As I got older, with more successes and more perspective to my credits, answering such mirror on the wall questions actually became harder. It didn't stop my leader from asking for feedback but perhaps, my age and experience lessened the chances that my advice could be dismissed as immature or lacking in context. Whether asked in public or private, providing consul or advice became more risky, and consequences more costly, both to my leadership and to me. Certainly, the questions were broader and more strategic; there was more at stake. But there could be prices to pay at the personal and relational levels, as well. Sometimes it was at the cost of friendship, or access to the inner circle. The price of honest feedback might manifest in anger or resentment.

If in the role of a follower who is subordinate but close to the leader's equal, the information, no matter how carefully and tactfully packaged, might be received never-the-less as biting criticism. For me, even if I considered the leader a close, trusted friend, such feedback chipped away at my leader's acceptance of me. Even the strongest leader has insecurities, and except for those rare ones with a genuine grain of self-awareness and a minimal dose of self-omnipotence, the desire to validate a chosen course of action is only human nature. But be especially wary of the weak leader or those with agendas you don't see. Those with fragile confidence, or unstable support, either from above them or from below, are looking to shore up weak columns and patch seeps and leaks. If your advice comes across as too strong of a counter argument, perceived as resistance or a possible threat to a leader's ability to implement his or her will, even trusted followers can find themselves ostracized, the butt end of derision, the target of a campaign to diminish their credibility, or even dismissed. It all comes down to how much trust you have in your leader and they in you.

Interestingly enough, once you are no longer the follower, perhaps now in the role of sage retiree, father-figure, or elderly statesman, such advice and consul, when asked for, is again more palatable. Possibly, it's because you have earned ultimate credibility in the eyes of the asking leader. More likely, though, it's because you've digressed back to "cute." Your insight is again easily dismissed as coming from a "nice old man [or lady] who just doesn't understand," or your information can be caveated as "not necessarily applicable today."

Tenet 36
Education and elocution

If Chapter Two is to be believed, every follower has a choice to follow or not follow their leader, and therefore every follower shares some responsibility for consequences. If every follower is duty-bound to future followers to consider the objectives of their leader's leaders (sometimes called "the institution," or "stockholder," or obliquely "the higher ups"); AND if a good follower is expected -- as mentioned in Tenet 4 – to do the right thing quietly; AND if it's not wise or in the follower's best interest to die for stupid causes as mentioned in Tenet 22, then every follower must constantly sharpen two tools in their in utility belt: education and elocution.

Jacque Ellul wrote in his book about propaganda ("Propaganda: The Formation of Men's Attitudes," Vintage Press, 1973) that to be effective, propaganda must be complete. In other words, it can have no dissenters. For a leader's idea to evolve into a movement, the leader must convince everyone that the idea is the best and only way. If not, then friction, time, and entropy usually make the idea difficult to implement. A powerful leader can compensate for this with sheer charisma, but it's easier to either start with a universally, undeniably-good concept or eliminate all alternate possibilities.

Have you ever wondered how the Nazi Party in the late 1930s and early 40s was able to convince so many people to do -- or allow the Nazis to do – unimaginable atrocities? Atrocities that Germany's average citizens might otherwise have rejected wholesale? They had to eliminate even vague hits of alternative endings to the Nazi Party's vision of the Third Reich, an imagined glorious era that surpassed in repression the domination and iron-fisted rule of the First and Second Reichs, the Holy Roman and Imperial German empires. Alternate currents of thought flowing through newspapers, synagogues, and universities were ruthlessly cut and cauterized, at first through intimidation with half-truths and ridicule, escalating to lies, isolation, and physical violence. Upstanding citizens and meek followers alike – probably all good people as

I think I found the problem.
The manual says to "disengage" the parking break,
not "disassemble."

individuals – didn't know or dared to question outloud what they were told. And
when those intimidation tactics didn't work fast enough, in the vacuum of dissent
the Nazi machine turned to death and extermination with impunity.

Ever wonder how Stalin was able to consolidate his power among the
wreckage of post-WWII Europe or how McCarthyism took hold in the U.S. in the
1950s? Ever wonder why Mao executed all the intellectuals and creative thinkers
in his 1950s purge, which Maoists labeled their "Great Leap Forward" and "the
Cultural Revolution" that followed in the mid-1960s?

Ever wonder if contemporary "ideals" inherent in racist, white supremacy,
Nazi, homophobic, or isolationist rhetoric could take hold in a true democracy?
If Jacque Ellul is correct, they can't as long as there are sufficient alternate or
dissenting ideas based on rational thought, and trusted lines of communication
that free-flow those ideas. Educated and eloquently-presented ideas. As a
leader or a movement pitches his, her, or its precepts, it is prudent for a good
follower to objectively analyze all sides of each argument; identify the omissions
and unknowns; look through the fog of half-truths and the friction inherent in
communicating less popular, dissenting, or newly discovered facts and opinion.

If you prefer to have lasting impact, be effective and useful to both your
leader and that leader's leaders, as a great follower, you must constantly improve
your understanding of real world surroundings, not as described or colored by a
leader who is trying to focus his or her phalanx on the flank of a problem, but as
a front line soldier sees it. A frontline soldier's very life may depend on the rise
of the countryside, distance to the tree line, or rockiness of its terrain; the length

of his pike vs. his enemy's; the resistance of humidity in the armor; or the ardent-ness, fanaticism, or lack of enthusiasm of the opposing force. Such situational awareness – for solders AND good followers -- must be built on a strong foundation of facts, not half-truths or false assumptions. Implied in this is the critical need to 1) have the reasoning skills and eloquence to analyze and articulate nuances; and 2) have reliable access to and knowledge of how to use two-way communication channels to transmit those facts, ideas (applied facts that others have come up with), observations, and alternate interpretations (facts turned on their heads and looked at another way).

In conclusion

During my first military assignment at the Air Force Academy, one of my bosses, a major and an academy graduate, told me that right or wrong, I'd learn something from his leadership style so I should pay attention. He also advised me to keep a journal and take notes about what I learned along the way. I've not only kept notes in a small, black leather diary, but I've since given small binders to "great followers" with whom I've had the privilege to work.

It is in a great follower's nature to be the grease, not the gears; to be the mortar, not the bricks. A machine cannot turn without lubrication; a wall will not stand without something to hold the pieces together. To become a great follower is as much a calling as choosing to become a great leader. It IS a choice and a noble one, although, perhaps destined to always be under-appreciated.

As you've probably figured out now that you've come to the end of the manual, there are many more than just these three dozen or so rules. And many less: since each are related and often overlap, they can be sliced any number of ways, reordered, grouped to make the list smaller, or fleshed out to make them more specific.

This is just my list based on the experiences of people I've talked to over the years, my research, and four decades of watching great—or at least interesting—leaders and followers. It reflects stories and lessons passed on in seminar discussions, office talk, and even over light conversation and bar drinks. All dutifully written down in that little black book. Some of the tenets in this book were distilled from followership decisions made in the heat of world-changing times that in retrospect made little difference in the end. We're all just small cogs in a much larger machine, after all. But some precepts, maybe many of them —probably most—evolved from seemingly mundane, one-on-one relationship decisions that historically turned out to be pivotal.

Tenets 37 and higher, well, those are yours to write. To repeat a line from Tenet 24: "Guess what? Tag, you're it!"

About the Author

Author and illustrator J. Michael Dumoulin has a Bachelor of Arts degree in Graphic Arts from Florida State University and a Bachelor of Science degree from the University of Florida. He received a Master of Science in Public Communications from Boston Universitiy and holds a Masters-equivalent in national strategy from the U.S. Air Force's Air War College.

Follower J. Michael Dumoulin has served at the Air Force Academy, the Pentagon's Office of the Secretary of the Air Force, Patrick and Peterson Air Force Bases, NASA's Marshall and Stennis space centers, and the agency's headquarters in Washington, D.C.

Manager J. Michael Dumoulin retired after 25 years with NASA, spending some of the time in space mission support roles but mostly leading a public outreach exhibits design and fabrication shop. Colonel J. Michael Dumoulin retired from the U.S. Air Force, spending his last six years in Homeland Security advising FEMA, generals, and governors' staffs on disaster preparedness and response.

For four years he served at the INFINITY Science Center, a medium-sized museum just east of New Orleans on the Gulf Coast in Mississippi, retiring as the not-for-profit's first director of strategic initiatives and development. To follow Author and Illustrator Dumoulin's latest projects and publications, check out jmichaeldumoulin.com.